The Blue Badge Guide's
LIVERPOOL
Quiz Book

The Blue Badge Guide's

LIVERPOOL
Quiz Book

Peter J. Colyer

The
History
Press

First published 2018

Reprinted 2019

The History Press
The Mill, Brimscombe Port
Stroud, Gloucestershire, GL5 2QG
www.thehistorypress.co.uk

British Library Cataloguing in Publication Data.

A catalogue record for this book is available from the British Library.

ISBN 978 0 7509 8447 8

Typesetting and origination by The History Press
Printed in Great Britain by TJ International Ltd, Padstow, Cornwall

Contents

Foreword

by Sara Wilde McKeown

Liverpool is a city of surprises, certainly for most people who visit it for the first time. Many visitors come with a fixed view of what it is going to be like and very quickly find that notion blown away. Prince Albert on opening the Albert Dock in Liverpool in 1846 said, 'I have heard of the great achievements of Liverpool but the reality far surpasses my expectation.' Today Liverpool continues to surprise and delight visitors from across the Globe.

A lot of people come because of their particular interest and often as ardent fans of either football or popular music. Once they are here they find there is so much more to this city and so much more to do and to see. The usual complaint is that they have not planned to spend enough time here! However, it's always good to have a reason to return and Liverpool provides you with reasons in abundance.

Liverpool is now very much on the tourist map – a visitor destination – whether they come by coach, train, plane, cruise ship or independently. This book opens up the city to new visitors in a way that is enjoyable and fun. It sets intriguing challenges to even the most regular visitors and encourages them to explore this fascinating city in even more depth in the company of one of its well-qualified Blue or Green Badge Guides.

Once visited and explored I hope Liverpool exceeds your expectations also.

Sara Wilde McKeown
Chair
Liverpool City Region Visitor Economy Board

Introduction

Liverpool, a provincial city in the north-west of England, has a worldwide reputation for football and The Beatles. Indeed, we are told, it is one or both of these that attract most of our overseas visitors. However, once visitors arrive they are stunned by a city they did not expect.

The city's architecture makes an immediate impression. Liverpool has twenty-seven Grade I listed buildings. Its museums and art galleries are national museums and house collections of international importance. The Walker Art Gallery is often referred to as the 'National Gallery of the North' and there is also a Tate Gallery.

Liverpool's reputation for popular music is second to none, but it is also the home of Britain's longest-established classical orchestra, the Royal Liverpool Philharmonic Orchestra, founded in 1840, the first to be patronised by royalty and which continues to produce concerts of international quality. You will find the best music of any genre somewhere in this city. Liverpool also has more live theatres than anywhere outside the capital and, as one of the first of Britain's multicultural cities, it can provide you with the highest quality dining in any culture you care to name.

But what really makes Liverpool stand out as a tourist destination is its people. It is not quite true that all Liverpudlians are either singers or comedians, but their sense of humour is legendary, and so is their friendliness and the welcome they give to visitors. It is said that if you ask for directions in this city the person you ask won't direct you, they will take you there!

I hope this quiz book will whet your appetite to come and see us, to explore the city and the region. I would strongly encourage you to engage one of our professional Blue or Green Badge tourist guides at some point in your visit. They will help you to make best use of your time here, show you places you would not otherwise find and share stories and information that will certainly enliven your stay. I guarantee that whilst you are here you will already be planning your return visit!

Peter J. Colyer
2018

Finding a Liverpool Blue or Green Badge guide

www.showmeliverpool.com/guides

About the Author

Peter J. Colyer qualified as a Liverpool City Region tourist guide after thirty-five years in teaching.

Born in Doncaster in South Yorkshire, he came to Liverpool to study history at the University of Liverpool in 1968. After training as a teacher he went on to teach history to secondary school students aged 11–19 for thirty-five years, becoming head of history, head of the humanities faculty and then deputy head of a large comprehensive school in Halifax for seventeen years. For his final three years he was associate head teacher. He gained a Master of Education degree from the University of Liverpool in 1989 and an M.A. in modern British history from the University of Leeds in 1996. He has been an active local preacher in the Methodist church since 1980.

Since retirement in 2007 he has divided his time between church work, principally managing four lay workers on behalf of the Wirral Methodist Circuit; and

tourist guiding. His interest and commitment to the study and teaching of history led him to become a volunteer room guide and education guide at Speke Hall, a sixteenth-century timber-framed manor house owned by the National Trust on the outskirts of Liverpool. He is also an education guide at Liverpool's Anglican Cathedral. In 2012–13 he took the opportunity to train as a professional tourist guide and achieved the Blue Badge, the highest tourist guiding qualification, from the Institute of Tourist Guiding. He has also trained to be a guide for the Port Sunlight Village Trust, as well as becoming an official York Minster guide in November 2014.

He enjoys travel and has learned a great deal about what makes a good tourist guide on guided tours in India, China, Thailand, Vietnam, Cambodia, Laos, USA, Australia, New Zealand, Egypt, Morocco and Tunisia, as well as Italy, Sicily and Russia.

This travel has taught him that people certainly want accurate information, but above all they want to know about people and their stories. So he delights in sharing the stories of the Liverpool region and its people, informed by his lifelong interest and study of history.

Peter is delighted to share his knowledge and passion for Liverpool and its region with you now. With considerably more than 220 facts, this book aims to inspire you to discover more of this amazing city in the company of a Blue or Green Badge guide!

peter.colyer@btinternet.com

Tour 1

The Old Seven Streets of Liverpool

When King John granted Liverpool a charter, or more accurately Letters Patent, in 1207 there were seven streets arranged in an H-shaped grid. These streets are still discernible today. Castle Street, Dale Street, Chapel Street and Tithebarn Street have retained their original names, whilst Bank Street is now Water Street, Mill Street is Old Hall Street, and Juggler Street is now High Street.

1. What will you now find on the site of the medieval castle in Derby Square?

2. If you look down Castle Street what is the magnificent domed building at the far end?

3. On the corner of Castle Street and Cook Street is a building with four Corinthian columns; which bank was this built for?

4. Walk down Cook Street past Union Court, which gives you a glimpse of Dickensian Liverpool on your left. On your right you will find 16 Cook Street. Why was this so unusual when it was built?

5. Along Tithebarn Street you will find an impressive building that was once a railway station. Which station?

6. Behind the Town Hall on Exchange Flags you will find the Nelson Memorial. Who are the prisoners in chains on the memorial?

7. Which sumptuously decorated arcade of shops and offices will you find linking Water Street with Brunswick Street?

8. No. 14 Water Street, on the corner with Covent Garden, is an amazing building. Why was it so controversial when it was first built?

9. How did Chapel Street get its name?

10. The word 'strand' means shore, but why is there a street called The Strand so far from the river?

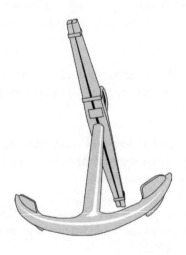

Answers – Tour 1

1. A magnificent statue, which is Liverpool's tribute to Victoria, Queen and Empress.

2. The Town Hall, designed by John Wood (1749-54); the dome was completed in 1802 and the portico completed in 1811 by James Wyatt.

3. The Bank of England. This was its first branch outside London. It was built 1845-48 and designed by Charles Cockerell.

4. Designed by Peter Ellis and built 1864-66. It was designed as offices and in order to allow as much light in as possible there is an amazing amount of plate glass to the proportion of stonework for the time. It was considered dangerously modern when it was built!

5. Exchange Station built in 1886 by the Lancashire & Yorkshire Railway Company, which ran trains from here north and to Scotland. The station closed in the 1970s and was redeveloped into offices known as Mercury Court, but the station façade has been retained.

6. Many people think they are slaves. However, they are French prisoners of war from the wars with

Napoleon at the beginning of the nineteenth century.

7. India Buildings completed in 1930 and designed by Arnold Thornely and Herbert J. Rowse.

8. This is Oriel Chambers designed by Peter Ellis and opened in 1864. It was controversial because of the enormous amount of glass in the building. This was to give as much light as possible into the building before electricity was widely used.

9. It was named because of the Chapel of St Mary del Key, first mentioned in 1257, which stood on the site of the present parish church of Our Lady and St Nicholas.

10. The river came right up to the present Strand until the late eighteenth century. All the docks and buildings to the river side of The Strand are built in the river!

Tour 2

UNESCO World Heritage City

You don't have to go to the Taj Mahal to visit a UNESCO World Heritage Site; Liverpool was designated a World Heritage City in 2004 because of its history as a maritime mercantile city. It is considered the supreme example of a commercial port at the time of Britain's greatest global influence. Liverpool has the biggest and most complete system of historic docks anywhere in the world. The World Heritage Site is spread over six locations in the city. See if you can identify them. These questions will get you started.

1. Liverpool was one of the first ports to have warehouses right on the dock side. This saved having to transport goods from the dock to warehouses in the city. Where will you find this?

2. Which impressive baroque building with its magnificent dome was built as a 'cathedral' to the trade that was coming in and out of the Port of Liverpool?

3. Which building reminds us that a port needs a financial infrastructure with powerful insurance companies to back up the shipping lines?

4. Where will you find a stunning arcade of shops and offices completed in 1930?

5. The merchants of Liverpool were not just focused on making money, they also had literary interests. What was built to prove this?

6. Which Victorian prime minister is quoted as saying 'Liverpool is the second city of the British Empire'? It earned him a statue at the front of St George's Hall.

7. The Bank of England decided that it needed a branch in the 'second city of the British Empire'. Where will you find this building?

8. Where will you find merchant houses and historic warehouses built in the eighteenth century?

9. Where will you find the largest brick warehouse in the world?

10. Which man-made waterway links three parts of the World Heritage Site?

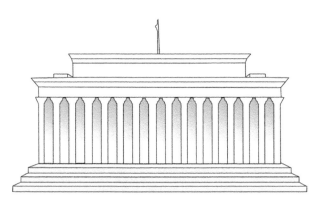

Answers - Tour 2

1. The Albert Dock, designed by Jesse Hartley and architect Philip Hardwick. It was built 1841–46 and opened by Prince Albert in 1846.

2. The Port of Liverpool Building on Canada Boulevard at the Pier Head. It was the headquarters of the Mersey Docks & Harbour Board. It was designed by architects Briggs & Wolstenholme with Thornely & Hobbs and built 1904–07.

3. The Royal Liver Building on Canada Boulevard at the Pier Head was built for the Royal Liver Insurance Company. It was designed by W. Aubrey Thomas and built in 1908–11. It was also innovative as it was the first reinforced concrete building of such a size.

4. India Buildings, which links Water Street and Brunswick Street. It was built for the shipping company Alfred Holt & Co., and was designed by Arnold Thornely and Herbert J. Rowse.

5. The Picton Reading Room in William Brown Street. It was designed by Cornelius Sherlock, built 1875–79 with more than a passing similarity to the circular Reading Room at the British Museum.

6. Benjamin Disraeli (1804–81), First Earl of Beaconsfield. He was prime minister from February to December 1868 and 1874–80.

7. On the corner of Cook Street and Castle Street, not far from the Town Hall. It was designed by C.R. Cockerell and was built in 1846–48.

8. Lower Duke Street in the area known as the Rope Walks. In Colquitt Street you will find the Royal Institution in a Paladian mansion built as a house for Thomas Parr in 1799. This gave the intelligentsia of Liverpool a special status.

9. The Stanley Dock Conservation Area to the north of the city. This is the Tobacco Warehouse.

10. The Leeds–Liverpool Canal constructed between 1770 and 1822. It is the longest single canal in the UK constructed by one company. In 2009 the £20 million Liverpool Canal Link extended the canal from the Stanley Dock, past the Three Graces on the Waterfront and into the Albert Dock and the Salthouse Dock, where canal boats can be moored.

Tour 3

The Albert Dock

A revolutionary design when it was opened in 1846, the restoration of the Albert Dock in the 1980s signalled the start of the regeneration of the city. Now it is a magnet for visitors with its shops, cafes, restaurants and museums as well as providing loft apartments.

1. How did the Albert Dock get its name?

2. Where will you learn all about the 'fab four'?

3. A branch of which world famous art gallery will you find here?

4. When he became engineer of the Liverpool docks, Jesse Hartley considered the system inefficient when goods had to be transported from the docks to the warehouses in the town. How was this dock built to cut down on that?

5. Why were 13,729 (or thereabouts) beech and elm trees needed before workers could even begin to build the dock?

6. Why did Jesse Hartley, the dock engineer, insist on building the warehouses with cast iron and brick?

7. All the pink Doric columns around the dock are made from cast iron. If you look carefully, however, you will find three grey columns together in one corner. Why is this?

8. Why do so many people who have never been to Liverpool before recognise the Dock Traffic Office with its stone Doric pillars and even talk about a weather map of Britain floating in the dock?

9. Condoleezza Rice, US Secretary of State, visited Liverpool in March 2006. Which museum did she describe as 'extraordinary'?

10. Why can you sometimes see canal narrow boats sailing through the Albert Dock?

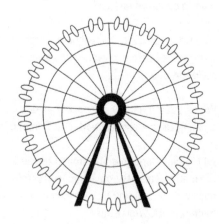

Answers – Tour 3

1. On 30 July 1846 Prince Albert, the husband of Queen Victoria, came to Liverpool to formally open the new dock and to give it his name.

2. The Beatles Story, a museum about the world famous group from Liverpool, is housed in the basement of the Britannia Pavilion in the Albert Dock. It opened in 1990.

3. Tate Liverpool was opened in the Albert Dock in 1988. It became the home of the National Collection of Modern Art in the North of England.

4. As the warehouses were on the quayside, goods could be unloaded from the ship straight into the bonded warehouses, thus saving a lot of time and energy.

5. The dock was built beyond the shoreline and well into the River Mersey. The trees were needed to give a solid foundation on the river bed on which to build it.

6. Too many of Liverpool's warehouses were vulnerable to fire. Hartley experimented and concluded that the most fire-resistant materials to build with were brick and cast iron.

7. These three columns are made of granite. The dock itself is built of granite and there was some left over. Hartley was determined not to waste it!

8. Granada TV Studios were located in the Dock Office Building between 1986 and 2006. It became famous because the *Richard and Judy Show* was produced there.

9. The International Slavery Museum, which is housed within the Maritime Museum in the Albert Dock.

10. The Leeds–Liverpool Canal, which originally terminated in the Stanley Dock, was extended in 2009 to enable boats to sail in front of the Three Graces, through the Albert Dock to moorings in the Salthouse Dock.

Tour 4

William Brown Street, the Cultural Quarter

By the middle of the nineteenth century Liverpool was famed as a place where the enterprising could make money and some of them certainly became very rich. The leading citizens wanted to show that they were cultured as well, so William Brown Street became the cultural quarter as buildings were built in the neo-classical style to house a music festival, a museum, a library and an art gallery. St George's Hall is considered a neo-classical masterpiece. One commentator says that the other buildings are not in the same league, but taken together as a piece of romantic classical urban scenery they have no equal in England.

1. St George's Hall was built in 1854 and is one of the finest neo-classical buildings in the world, but why was it built?

2. The floor in the concert hall is made of stunningly beautiful Minton tiles. Why can't you always see them?

3. In the concert hall there are statues of a number of outstanding men of the city who made their mark in the nineteenth century. There is now a statue of one woman. Who is she and what important contribution did she make to the city?

4. You will see Walker's Ales advertised on some of the finest pubs in the city. Has this anything to do with the Walker Art Gallery?

5. Why are the gardens behind St George's Hall, alongside William Brown Street, known as St John's Gardens?

6. Where will you find an outstanding collection of Ancient Egyptian antiquities?

7. Why might you have to walk over your favourite books to get into the Central Library?

8. Where can you go to imagine you are in the Reading Room of the British Museum?

9. Where will you get a good panoramic view of William Brown Street and the surrounding area?

10. Just before you enter William Brown Street on the right-hand side is a recently erected memorial in the shape of a massive drum with ninety-six names on it. Why was this placed here?

Answers – Tour 4

1. To house a tri-annual music festival and to provide court rooms for the newly established assize courts.

2. They are covered with deep wood blocks and are only uncovered on special occasions as it is very expensive to do this.

3. Kitty Wilkinson (1786–1860). Kitty believed soiled clothing was not healthy at a time when disease was killing many people in Liverpool. She opened her own home to enable the poor to wash their clothing. She inspired the creation of the network of wash houses throughout the city.

4. Yes. Andrew Barclay Walker, who built some of the best pubs in the city, was elected Mayor of Liverpool in 1873 and gave £20,000 towards the building of the public art gallery that now bears his name.

5. When St George's Hall was built St John's church stood in what is now the gardens. This was a Gothic building built in 1775–83 and demolished in 1898.

6. The World Museum built in 1857–60 in the neo-classical style and rebuilt in 1963–69 after war damage.

7. The walkway leading into the stunningly refurbished Central Library has the titles of some famous books carved into the stone. See how many of them you have read!

8. The Picton Reading Room in the Central Library is a rotunda just like the Reading Room in the British Museum. It was designed by Cornelius Sherlock and built in 1875–79. Be careful about entering this room, its atmosphere has the power to draw you into one of its books and you will be there for hours!

9. When you enter the Central Library the new atrium definitely has the wow factor. Go up the escalators or take the lift to the top floor. There you will find a viewing platform that will give you stunning views of St George's Hall and the surrounding buildings, as well as a distant view of the Three Graces and other landmark buildings.

10. This is one of the memorials to the ninety-six football fans killed at the football match at the Hillsborough stadium in Sheffield in 1989. This event and its aftermath had such a profound effect on the people of Liverpool that you will find other memorials to it as you explore the city.

Tour 5

The Ropewalks
of Liverpool

There are several long, narrow straight streets that
go downhill in the city towards the Waterfront. In the
eighteenth and nineteenth centuries rope for the rigging
of sailing ships was manufactured in Liverpool. This
required long, narrow stretches where ropes made from
hemp could be spun by rope makers walking backwards
from a spinning wheel. The rope makers have long since
gone but this group of streets where they spun the hemp
is still known as The Ropewalks – Bold Street, Wood
Street, Fleet Street, Seel Street and Duke Street.

1. John Bellingham lived on Duke Street. He is unique in British history, for what violent achievement?

2. Nathaniel Hawthorne lodged at 186 Duke Street when he lived in Liverpool in the 1860s. Why was he here?

3. You will find a very fine sandstone building on the corner of Duke Street and Slater Street. It dates from 1800, but why was it built?

4. Just off Duke Street is Colquitt Street and here you will find the Royal Institution. Why has this been a very influential building in the history of the city?

5. Further up Duke Street you will find Dukes Terrace behind the main street. These homes have been converted into through houses for modern living but why do they remind visitors of a darker time for Liverpool's poor?

6. There is a statue of William Huskisson opposite Dukes Terrace. He is remembered in Liverpool because of the way he died – how?

7. At the bottom of Bold Street there is a grand Greek revival building from 1802. What was this built for?

8. Why is one of the streets that turns into Bold Street known as Concert Street?

9. Numbers 14–16 Bold Street date from 1848–61 and have very special plate glass windows. Does this mean the building has a distinguished past?

10 If you look above the shop fronts you will see the original style of the buildings. No. 58 Bold Street stands out for which style of architecture?

Answers – Tour 5

1. He is the only man to have assassinated a British prime minister. He shot Spencer Percival in the lobby of the House of Commons in 1812.

2. He was the American Consul.

3. It was built as the Union News Room, a gentlemen's club where patrons could read the newspapers. In the 1850s it became the town's first public library. Only the façade is now original.

4. Built as a private residence in 1799, it was taken over by the Liverpool Royal Institution in 1815 and become the centre for the promotion and study of literature, science and the arts in Liverpool.

5. These are the only surviving back-to-back houses in Liverpool. At the end of the nineteenth century houses such as this would have accommodated thousands of poor people in appalling conditions.

6. He was a Liverpool MP and a senior member of the British Government in the 1820s. He sadly became the first fatal victim of a railway accident when he attended the opening of the Liverpool to Manchester railway in 1830.

7. This is the Lyceum. It was built to house the first gentlemen's subscription library in England, which had been established in 1757. It closed in 1942.

8. On the corner of Bold Street and Concert Street is a building that used to be the Halles Des Modes because it was a music hall.

9. Yes it does. This building was built for Cripps, a fashion store selling ladies clothes and shawls that was the first of its kind. Miss Tinnie was a celebrated patron of this shop. Bold Street in the nineteenth century was known for fashion stores and furriers.

10. It was built in the Arts and Crafts style, a mid-nineteenth century attempt to return to a style of living before the coming of the factories. Such a style was a myth but it produced some interesting buildings.

Tour 6

Rodney Street

One of the most prestigious streets in Liverpool, Rodney Street was named to commemorate Admiral Lord Rodney's naval victory at the Battle of Cape St Vincent (1780) in the American War of Independence. It was built in the late eighteenth century and into the first decade of the nineteenth century. Thus Rodney Street boasts both Georgian and Regency architecture. According to one expert it represents 'Georgian architecture at its best'.

1. Which great Victorian prime minister was born at No. 62?

2. Inspect the brass plates on many of the doors. Why is Rodney Street known as the Harley Street of Liverpool?

3. Which famous manager of popular Liverpool music stars was born behind the door of No. 4?

4. Where will you find a time capsule that was the home and studio of a renowned society photographer?

5. Rodney Street is famous for its Georgian and Regency houses. Can you tell the difference?

6. Where will you find a plate marking the birthplace of a notable Victorian lady who is also commemorated in the Noble Women window of the Anglican Cathedral?

7. What is the link between the very grand St Andrew's church and the shipbuilders on the Birkenhead side of the River Mersey?

8. Will you be spooked by the ghoulish story about the pyramid in the graveyard of St Andrew's church?

9. No. 11 was the birthplace of a distinguished Liverpool surgeon who used his experiences at sea in the Second World War to write a book that became a popular film starring Jack Hawkins. Do you know which author and which film?

10. Look carefully at the plaque outside No. 4. Which important person lived here from 1790–1840?

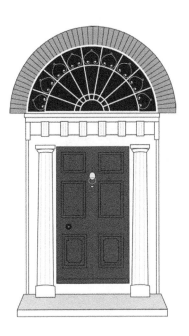

Answers - Tour 6

1. William Ewart Gladstone on 29 December 1809.

2. A number of medical practices have their consulting rooms in Rodney Street.

3. Brian Epstein, The Beatles' manager. He was born here in 1934 when the house was a private nursing home.

4. No. 59, home of Edward Chambre Hardman and his wife, Margaret. The company was Burrrell & Hardman, which originated in Bold Street. It is now looked after by the National Trust and is open to the public.

5. Regency houses (*c.* 1790–1830s) are later than Georgian houses (*c.* 1720s–1790s). The Regency houses in Rodney Street have iron railings and iron work on balconies, semicircular fanlights over the doors, half-basements and steps up to the front doors. They also have higher windows in the first and second floors compared with the ground floor.

6. This is at No. 9, the birthplace of Anne Jemima Clough (1820–92). She was a pioneer of female higher education and the first principal of

Newnham College, Cambridge. Her brother, Arthur Clough (1819–61), was also born here. He was a celebrated poet and assistant to Florence Nightingale.

7. The Laird family established ship building on the Wirral banks of the River Mersey in the 1820s. The company had become Cammell Laird by the end of the nineteenth century. They were members at St Andrews, a Scottish Presbyterian church, and contributed to the cost of the building.

8. The story is that William Mackenzie, a gambling man, sold his soul to the Devil, but the Devil could only claim it when he was put under the ground. So his body has been seated inside the granite pyramid ever since his death in 1851. His ghost is said to haunt Rodney Street.

9. Nicholas Monsarrat was born on 22 March 1910. His book about the Atlantic convoys in the Second World War was made into the film *The Cruel Sea*.

10. James Maury, first US Consul to Liverpool. He was appointed by George Washington.

Tour 7

Hope Street

Liverpool's two cathedrals are linked by a street called Hope. However, Hope Street has been there for many years before either cathedral was ever thought of. It is now a centre for music and drama of the highest standard as well as boasting top-quality restaurants and cafes.

1. Where will you find a permanent pile of suitcases?

2. Where will you find one of the most richly decorated gentlemen's toilets in the city?

3. Which is the home of the longest established classical orchestra in the country?

4. Where would you have found John Lennon and his art school friends drinking when they probably should have been in lessons?

5. Which two Beatles went to school just around the corner from Hope Street?

6. Which two senior churchmen have a joint memorial outside the London Carriage Works?

7. There is a restaurant housed in a very grand building that was built in the nineteenth century to educate children with a particular disability, what was it?

8. Which very grand building was purchased by George Holt and turned into the first girls' school in the city?

9   Which building won the Sterling prize for architecture in 2014?

10. Where did John Lennon and his art school mates have a flat that he left to go to Hamburg in 1960?

Answers – Tour 7

1. Where Hope Street meets the top of Mount Street. Search the luggage for the names of famous people associated with Hope Street.

2. The Philharmonic Dining Rooms. The furniture in the gents toilets is not porcelain – it's marble! Ladies are allowed in to see it – by arrangement.

3. The Philharmonic Hall, the home of the Royal Liverpool Philharmonic Orchestra, founded in 1840. The original hall was opened in 1849 but burnt down in 1933. The present art deco building was opened in 1939.

4. Ye Cracke, 13 Rice Street, just off Hope Street. You will find a plaque to commemorate a pledge that Lennon and three of his friends, who styled themselves The Dissenters, made to put Liverpool 'on the map'.

5. Paul McCartney and George Harrison went to what was then The Institute, a boys' school in Mount Street. It is now the Liverpool Institute for Performing Arts (LIPA), established by McCartney.

6. Bishop David Sheppard and Archbishop Derek Warlock. Their embossed figures are surrounded

by many of the newspaper headlines that their activities and campaigns generated.

7. The Blind School, which is on the corner of Hope Street and Hardman Street. It was built in 1849–51.

8. Blackburne House, which is in Hope Street between Blackburne Place and Falkner Street. Built in 1788, it became a school in 1844 and was enlarged in 1874–76. The school closed in 1986 and it was transformed into a women's training centre in 1994 with a café in the basement.

9. The Everyman Theatre.

10. No. 3 Gambier Terrace, overlooking the Anglican Cathedral.

Tour 8

A Ribbon of Parks

For a city whose main focus is the river, Liverpool has an amazing quantity of parkland. Inspired by the builders of private parks, the local councils of Liverpool and Birkenhead saw the opportunity to improve the living conditions of the workers by providing open spaces for them to enjoy their time off. Living conditions for working-class families in the middle of the nineteenth century were very poor, and as a result preventable diseases such as cholera and typhoid were rife. Building parks was seen as one way to tackle this.

1. If you want a break from shopping in the city centre where would you find the opportunity to relax in a green space dedicated to a Liverpool war hero?

2. In 1984 a vast rubbish dump to the south of the city was transformed into an attraction that welcomed 3.4 million visitors from all over the world. What was it?

3. Which of Merseyside's parks provided the inspiration for the design of Central Park in New York?

4. Where will you find the spectacular Victorian Palm House (built 1896), full of exotic plants and guarded by statues of great adventurers from history?

5. Which was the first park to be built in Liverpool? It was the inspiration of Richard Vaughan Yates and originally a private park.

6. Liverpool Corporation built a 'ribbon of parks' around the edges of what was then the extent of Liverpool: Newsham Park in 1868, Stanley Park in 1870, and Sefton Park in 1872. Why did they do this?

7. Where will you find Liverpool's oldest structures?

8. From here you will get a spectacular view of the city and the river, famously enjoyed by a prince, as well as enjoying a large green open space. Where is it?

9. The gardens in the shell of which church provide an oasis of calm in the city centre?

10. In which park will you find the splendid Gladstone Conservatory, which has recently been restored?

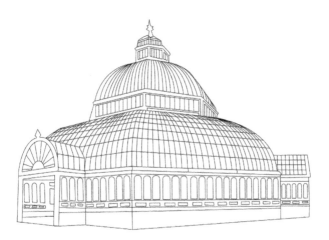

Answers - Tour 8

1. Chavasse Park is on the top of the Liverpool One shopping centre. It is dedicated to Noel Chavasse (1884–1917) who won the Military Cross and the Victoria Cross twice in the First World War, the only person to do so in that conflict.

2. Liverpool's International Garden Festival. The Festival Gardens are still worth a visit.

3. Birkenhead Park, which was opened in 1847. Frederick Law Olmsted, known as the 'father of landscape architecture' in the USA, visited Birkenhead Park in the 1850s and was inspired by it to create Central Park.

4. Sefton Park in south Liverpool.

5. Princes Park at the end of Princes Road.

6. To improve public health. At the time many of the working people were housed in insanitary courts and back-to-back houses in the centre of Liverpool. The parks were designed to give them the opportunity for fresh air and exercise.

7. At Calderstones Park in south Liverpool. The Calder Stones are six surviving stones from a Neolithic

burial chamber from 5,000 years ago and they have circles and spiral markings. They are now in one of the surviving glasshouses of the botanic gardens.

8. Everton Park. This was created after the demolition of streets of terraced houses in the 1960s and 1970s. This was where Prince Rupert brought his troops in the English Civil War in his attempt to capture Liverpool, which was held by the Parliamentarians.

9. St Luke's church on Berry Street.

10. Stanley Park. It was donated to the city by Henry Yates Thompson in 1900.

Tour 9

Two Cathedrals and Other Places of Worship

Liverpool is famous for its two cathedrals, both built in the twentieth century in very different architectural styles. They face each other from the two ends of Hope Street, a concrete symbol of the harmony between the faith communities of the city pioneered by Bishop Sheppard and Archbishop Warlock in the 1970s, known as the 'Mersey Miracle'. Although the cathedrals dominate the city, it has a wealth of beautiful religious buildings that evidence its ethnic and cultural diversity.

1. Which is the largest cathedral in the UK and one of the largest in the world?

2. Which cathedral can seat more than 2,000 people and yet no one is very far from the altar?

3. Why does one of the cathedrals have an enormous network of crypts beneath it that is far bigger than the actual cathedral itself?

4. In which building will you find the highest and heaviest set of church bells in the world?

5. Where will you find a synagogue that is so elaborately decorated inside that it is a Grade I listed building?

6. Where will you find a domed Byzantine-style Greek Orthodox church with five cupolas?

7. On Princes Road you will find a splendid spire. The church itself is in ruins but when it was built in the nineteenth century it was known as the 'Welsh Cathedral'. Why did Liverpool need such a large Welsh church?

8. Where will you find Derby mouse, much beloved by children? They all have to touch him, so he shines like gold.

9. Where will you find the 'sailors' church'? Why isn't it as old as it looks?

10. Where will you find the oldest original chapel in Liverpool?

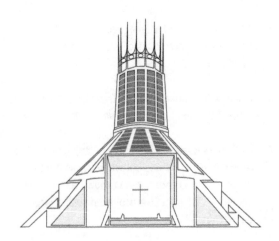

Answers – Tour 9

1. This is Liverpool's Anglican Cathedral. Its size is overtaken only by cathedrals in New York, Milan and Seville. The largest church in the world, St Peter's Basilica in Rome, is, of course, not a cathedral.

2. Liverpool's Metropolitan Cathedral. This is achieved by its circular design. It was designed by Sir Frederick Gibberd and was built in 1962–67.

3. Liverpool's Metropolitan Cathedral. The original design for the cathedral by Sir Edwin Lutyens would have made it the largest cathedral in the world. The enormous crypts were built in the 1930s but the war brought the building to a halt. After the war it was eventually decided to build a much smaller cathedral.

4. Liverpool's Anglican Cathedral. If you pay to go to the top of the tower for probably the best panoramic view of the region, you will walk through the bell chamber and wonder how they got such heavy bells up this high.

5. On Princes Road. This building looks quite modest from the outside but inside the spectacular decoration is awe-inspiring.

6. You will find the Greek Orthodox church of St Nicholas at the Parliament Street end of Princes Road. It was built in 1865–70.

7. Many Welsh people came to Liverpool and settled here in order to build houses. Most of the terraced houses in the city were built by the Welsh. At one point Liverpool had a larger Welsh population than any city in Wales.

8. You will find this on the memorial to Lord Derby in the Derby Transept of the Anglican Cathedral.

9. This is the church of Our Lady and St Nicholas at the end of Chapel Street on what used to be the banks of the river. Although there has been a chapel on this site since at least as early as 1257, the current church suffered from heavy bombing in the Second World War and has been rebuilt. The tower dates from 1814.

10. Dingle's ancient chapel at the corner of Park Road and Ullet Road. The chapel was completed in 1618 and was partly rebuilt in 1774. It is one of the oldest non-conformist chapels in the UK.

Tour 10

A Magical Mystery Tour

Liverpool is probably most famous nationally and internationally because of The Beatles. Paul McCartney, John Lennon, George Harrison and Ringo Starr were promoted as the 'fab four' by their manager Brian Epstein in 1962 and they dominated the popular music charts until they dissolved the band in 1969. It is often claimed that they transformed popular music, especially the songs of Lennon and McCartney. Their music continues to be popular with succeeding generations and fans of all ages coming to Liverpool on a pilgrimage to see where it all began and the city that inspired the music.

1. The Cavern Club, a jazz club started in a cellar in 1957, was where The Beatles became famous. In which narrow street will you find it?

2. Where might you see a 'barber showing photographs', 'a banker with a motorcar' and 'a pretty nurse selling poppies from a tray'?

3. A larger than life sculpture of The Beatles was commissioned by the owners of the Cavern Club and unveiled in 2015. Where will you find it?

4. 'All the lonely people.' The singer Tommy Steele created a very evocative statue of a lonely character from a Beatles song. Who is she and where is the statue?

5. In the basement of which pub will you find murals by Stuart Sutcliffe of The Beatles and some that are probably by John Lennon?

6. 'Strawberry Fields Forever!' But where will you find them?

7. No. 20 Forthlin Road and Mendips on Menlove Avenue are preserved by the National Trust as the childhood homes of two of the Beatles. Which ones?

8. Which night club saw a failed audition by The Beatles in 1960 and later performances by The Rolling Stones, Bob Dylan and Judy Garland?

9. 'Case Histories', the art installation of concrete suitcases at the Anglican Cathedral end of Hope Street, features John Lennon, Paul McCartney and George Harrison. What was their link with Hope Street?

10. 'Do you want to know a secret?' is on The Beatles' 1963 LP *Please Please Me*. It was written by John Lennon after he moved into No. 36 Falkner Street in August 1962. What was the secret?

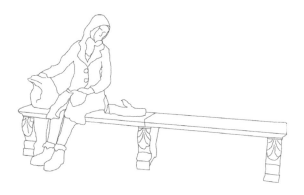

Answers - Tour 10

1. Mathew Street, with only one 'T'! It is a very narrow street, easy to miss, between North John Street and Stanley Street. Now it is full of Beatles-themed attractions.

2. Penny Lane, made famous by The Beatles in their song released in 1967. More accurately it will be the roundabout at the end of Penny Lane off Allerton Road in Mossley Hill.

3. On Canada Boulevard, looking towards the ferry terminal and with their backs to the Three Graces.

4. Eleanor Rigby (1966). The statue sits on a stone bench in Stanley Street.

5. The Jacaranda, No. 23 Slater Street. This is one of the places members of The Beatles went during their student days – they went for the bacon butties. They also played there several times in 1960.

6. Strawberry Fields' gates are on Beaconsfield Road in Allerton. The song released in 1967 is about the thickly wooded grounds of the Strawberry Fields Salvation Army hostel behind John Lennon's childhood home.

7. No. 20 Forthlin Road was the home of Paul McCartney and Mendips, the home of John Lennon. You can visit them but only using the National Trust minibus.

8. The Blue Angel, No. 108 Seel Street. The Beatles failed an audition there in 1960 in a bid to be the support band for a tour by Billy Fury, who was then a much more famous Liverpool performer.

9. John Lennon attended the art college which was right next to the suitcases. Paul McCartney and George Harrison went to school at The Institute, the building with the columned entrance that is in view of the suitcases down Mount Street.

10. A double secret. This was Brian Epstein's flat where he took his lovers. Epstein lent it to Lennon for his honeymoon after he married Cynthia, on condition the marriage was kept secret; marriage didn't fit the image of The Beatles being promoted by Epstein.

Tour 11

A Pub Crawl

Liverpool offers a wide choice of public houses in which
to meet friends and relax after a hard day's work, or a
hard day's sightseeing. They range from the large and
grandiose to the small and intimate, and many of them
have a story or two to tell as well.

1. How did the Pump House Inn at the Albert Dock get its name?

2. The Baltic Fleet at Wapping is a popular tourist destination. Its cellars contain mysterious tunnels and hideaways. Why should drinkers have been more wary, certainly up to the First World War?

3. Which elaborately built pub next to the Adelphi Hotel was patronised by stars such as Mae West, Charlton Heston and Bing Crosby?

4. Why was The Grapes pub in Mathew Street very popular with The Beatles, other performers and audiences from the Cavern Club?

5. Where might you be forgiven for thinking you are in church rather than in a pub?

6. Which is Liverpool's oldest public house?

7. Which pub has stood in splendid isolation since all the buildings around it were destroyed in the bombing of 1941? It is next to a car park that is one of the last surviving bomb sites in the city.

8. Which famous son of Liverpool said, 'the worst thing about being famous is you can't go for a pint in the Phil'?

9. The Irish have made a major contribution to Liverpool's culture, and not least to its pubs. If you were after the Irish 'black stuff' what would you be seeking and where would you find it in its most authentic setting?

10. Which small pub has a small snug known as the 'War Office' that has listed status? It is also famous as one of the places John Lennon and his mates drank when they should have been attending to their studies at the art college.

Answers – Tour 11

1. It was built as the Albert Dock Hydraulic Power centre in 1878. It housed an enormous steam engine that powered a steam-powered hydraulic system that did all the heavy lifting in the Albert Dock. It became a pub in 1986.

2. It was notorious for 'crimps'. They would trick young men into signing up for long and dangerous voyages on merchant ships using bribery and intimidation, or they would drug their drink.

3. The Vines, No. 81 Lime Street, sometimes known as the 'Big House'.

4. The Cavern Club did not have an alcohol licence in those days and only served coca-cola or coffee. If you wanted an alcoholic drink you had to go down to The Grapes.

5. Alma de Cuba, St Peter's church in Seel Street. This was built as a Roman Catholic church in 1788 and served as such until 1993, when it was deconsecrated and became a pub. As a Grade II listed building, many of the original church features remain in place.

6. Ye Hole in Ye Wall, in Hackins Hey. It is reputed to date from 1726.

7. The Pig and Whistle on the corner of Chapel Street and Covent Garden.

8. John Lennon. He meant the Philharmonic Dining Rooms in Hope Street – not the Philharmonic Hall.

9. The 'black stuff' would be Guinness and you would find it in its most Irish settings in the Pogue Mahone in Seel Street and Shenanigans in Tithebarn Street. But remember to drink responsibly.

10. Ye Cracke, No. 13 Rice Street, just off Hope Street. The 'War Office' got its name because older drinkers would meet here to discuss the progress of the Boer War (1899–1902).

Tour 12

Listed Buildings

The listing of important buildings has its origins in the Second World War when the Luftwaffe seemed to be targeting the most important ones. The government sent out a team of civil servants to list and grade Britain's most historically significant buildings, and this continued after the war as a system to protect and preserve them. A very small proportion of listed buildings are classified as Grade I, yet Liverpool has twenty-seven of them, together with a lot that are graded II*. See how many you can see during your visit.

1. Which cluster of warehouses built on the river and opened by the Prince Consort in 1846 are Grade I listed buildings?

2. Which Grade I listed building welcomes you to Liverpool whether you arrive by train at Lime Street station or through the Birkenhead Tunnel?

3. Which Grade I listed building is regarded as the symbol of the city and welcomes visitors who arrive by sea?

4. Which Grade I listed building broods over the whole city from its elevated position on a sandstone ridge?

5. Which Grade II listed buildings will help you to breathe if you make a car journey to Birkenhead?

6. Which Grade I listed building is the world's first iron-framed, glass-walled building, built in 1864?

7. Where will you find a Grade I listed building whose decoration is influenced by the Moorish style?

8. Which Grade I listed building was built as a school in 1716–25 and is now a centre for the arts in the city?

9. Which Grade I listed building is the setting for civic ceremonies and celebrations and has seen many sporting trophies displayed on its balcony?

10. Which Grade I listed building was the first branch of the country's most important bank to be built outside London?

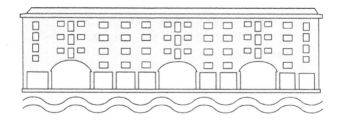

Answers - Tour 12

1. The Albert Dock, designed by Jesse Hartley and architect Philip Hardwick in 1841–46. It was closed in 1972 and reopened in 1988.

2. St George's Hall. The architect was Harvey Lonsdale Elmes with C.R. Cockerell, and it was built in 1840–54.

3. The Royal Liver Building designed by architect W. Aubrey Thomas, built in 1908–11. It was reputed to be the tallest office building in Europe between 1911 and 1932.

4. Liverpool's Anglican Cathedral. Designed by architect Sir Giles Gilbert Scott, it was built between 1904 and 1978.

5. The Mersey Tunnel ventilation towers. There are six of these, built between 1931 and 1934, on the two sides of the river for the Birkenhead Road Tunnel. The architect was Herbert Rowse, who also designed the entrances to the tunnel. See if you can find them all.

6. Oriel Chambers on Water Street. Designed by Peter Ellis, it was too modern for many at the time, but

see what you think. Peter Ellis also designed
No. 16 Cook Street, which is Grade II* listed.

7. Princes Road synagogue. It was designed by W. &
    G. Audsley and built in 1872–74. Opposite you will
    find the spire and the shell of what was known as
    the 'Welsh Cathedral'. This was also designed by
    Audsley and built in 1868.

8. The Bluecoat between College Lane and School
    Lane. The shell is original Queen Anne style, while
    the interior has been adapted for contemporary
    use down the years. The building and its gardens
    provide an oasis of peace in the centre of the city.

9. The Town Hall at the end of Castle Street. It was
    designed by architects John Wood the Elder of
    Bath and James Wyatt between 1749 and 1811.

10. The Bank of England building in Castle Street.
    It was designed by architect C.R. Cockerill in
    1845–48.

Tour 13

Tunnels, Bridges and Railways

Liverpool has always been at the forefront of innovations in transport, especially with regard to canals and railways. The River Mersey is the lifeblood of the city, but crossing it has always presented a challenge down the centuries and different solutions have been found in each generation.

1. Why were the telegraph wires into Albion House (now No. 30 James Street Hotel next to James Street Station) hot in April 1912?

2. William Huskisson, MP for Liverpool and colonial secretary, was killed in 1830. What was historic about his death?

3. When the Liverpool to Manchester railway was being planned they weren't sure a locomotive could be made that would be powerful enough. What settled the problem?

4. The traditional way to cross the Mersey is by ferry. Who operated the first ferries?

5. Regular and reliable ferries date from the 1820s. What innovation made this possible?

6. The two road tunnels under the river are Queensway, opened in 1934, and Kingsway, opened in 1971. Who opened them?

7. There is an even older tunnel under the river opened by the Prince of Wales in 1886. Can you name it?

8. Liverpool people still talk about the 'Docker's Umbrella'. What was that?

9. Where is the first bridge to cross the River Mersey?

10. Liverpool's Airport, opened in the 1920s, was known as Speke Airport for many years. It is now named after one of the city's most famous sons. Which one?

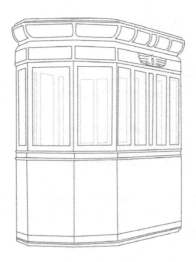

Answers – Tour 13

1. This was the headquarters of the White Star shipping line. Bad news was coming in about their newest ship on its maiden voyage; the *Titanic*. Lots of people from Liverpool worked on the ship.

2. His was the first fatal accident in the history of the railways. He was attending the opening of the first passenger railway line, the Liverpool to Manchester Railway.

3. The Rainhill Trials of 1829. George Stephenson's locomotive *Rocket* proved that a steam locomotive could pull a train at 27mph. Edgehill Station is the oldest railway station still operating in the world.

4. It is believed to have been the monks of the Benedictine priory of Birkenhead in the twelfth century.

5. The introduction of steam ferries; a regular service has operated ever since. Wealthy businessmen started to live on the Wirral side of the river and take the ferry to their businesses in Liverpool. It is still worth taking the ferry today to get stunning views of the Liverpool Waterfront.

6. Queensway was opened in 1934 by King George V and Kingsway was opened in 1971 by Queen Elizabeth II. Merseyside logic is not always the same as everyone else's!

7. The railway tunnel. However, this wasn't a great success because the steam engines made for an unpleasant ride, however, in 1903 the line was electrified and it is still the most common way to cross the river. Notice on the tower of Hamilton Square Station in Birkenhead the writing 'Frequent Electric Trains!' And they still are.

8. The Overhead Railway, the world's first electrically powered elevated railway system. Officially opened to the public in 1893, it ran from Seaforth in north Liverpool to Dingle in the south and provided spectacular views over the docks. It closed in 1956 and was dismantled in 1957. You can see original carriages in the Museum of Liverpool.

9. The Runcorn Bridge, later known as the Silver Jubilee Bridge, was opened in 1961. Just beyond that is the multi-million pound Mersey Gateway opened in autumn 2017.

10. John Lennon. The airport was officially renamed in July 2001 by Yoko Ono.

Tour 14

Statues

Liverpool has a long tradition of raising statues to commemorate men and women born in the city who have gone on to make a name for themselves and the city, or people who have come to Liverpool from elsewhere and made a major contribution to the city itself. This tradition has continued through into recent years, indeed some of the people commemorated are still alive.

1. 'In my Liverpool home ... we meet under a statue exceedingly bare!' So goes the song, but where is the statue?

2. Which Liverpool comedian and legendary female MP from the city are found greeting each other?

3. Which two brothers will you find outside Primark in Church Street? The building that houses Primark was built as the Littlewoods store.

4. Where will you find the young Queen Victoria and Prince Albert on horseback?

5. Which British monarch will you find in her pomp on the site of Liverpool's castle in Derby Square?

6. Which 1960s pop singer from Liverpool will you find with arms outstretched in front of the original entrance to the Cavern Club in Mathew Street?

7. Where will you find the four Beatles? See if you can spot them underneath all the tourists who want their pictures taken with them.

8. Where will you find the statue of Liverpool's legendary Kitty Wilkinson (1786–1860)?

9. Why will you find a statute of Captain F.J. Walker (1896–1944) on the Waterfront directly in front of the Port Authority building?

10. Billy Fury (1940–83) is another singing son of Liverpool who is remembered fondly. Where is his statue?

Answers – Tour 14

1. This is 'Liverpool Resurgent', or 'Dickie Lewis' as many Liverpudlians refer to him. He is on the building that used to house Lewis's department store opposite the Adelphi Hotel on the corner of Ranelagh and Renshaw streets. The statue is 18ft high, dates from 1956 and is by Jacob Epstein.

2. Bessie Braddock and Sir Ken Dodd are to be found on the concourse of Lime Street Station.

3. Freeman Sir John Moores and Cecil Moores, respectively founder and director of the Littlewoods organisation and great benefactors of the city.

4. Outside St George's Hall and opposite Lime Street Station on St George's Plateau.

5. Queen Victoria, Queen and Empress (1837–1901).

6. Cilla Black (1943–2015). This statue was unveiled by her sons in January 2017.

7. On the Waterfront along Canada Boulevard between the Three Graces and the Mersey Ferry Terminal. Unveiled in December 2015, it was

donated by the owners of the famous Cavern Club and sculpted by Andrew Edwards.

8. St George's Hall. The statue joined the twelve Victorian and Edwardian men already commemorated there in September 2012. It was sculpted by Simon Smith. Wilkinson's work in opening her house for poor people to wash their clothes in the wake of the cholera epidemic of 1832 led to the establishment of public wash houses.

9. It is to celebrate him and his men of 36th Escort and 2nd Support Group and all those who fought in the Battle of the Atlantic in 1939–45. It was commissioned by Captain Walker Old Boys Association, sculpted by Tom Murphy and unveiled by the Duke of Edinburgh on 16 October 1998.

10. You will find him on the Waterfront in front of the pier master's house, usually with fresh flowers.

Tour 15

Sport and Leisure

Liverpool is world famous for its football teams because Premier League football matches are broadcast all over the world. Liverpool Football Club especially has a worldwide fan base and many pilgrims travel to pay homage at the home stadium. Merseyside has had success in other sports as well as providing venues for sporting events of national and international importance.

1. Which world famous horse race is run at Aintree Race Course in Liverpool in April each year?

2. Which park separates the two major Premier League football grounds?

3. Which football ground is nearest to the River Mersey?

4. 'Some people think that football is a matter of life and death. I can assure you that it is much more serious than that.' Who is famously credited with that statement?

5. Which football team plays at Prenton Park in Birkenhead?

6. Which county cricket team plays regularly in Liverpool?

7. Which of Liverpool's two Premier League football teams has been established the longest?

8. When the new multi-million pound shopping centre was opened in the centre of the city in 2008 it was called Liverpool One. When Everton FC opened their shop there how did they have fun with the name of the shop?

9. St Helen's is a town on the outskirts of Liverpool. It is famous for glass making and success in which sport?

10. Which two Liverpool area golf courses have hosted the Open Golf Championship?

Answers – Tour 15

1. The Grand National. First run in 1839 it is a handicap steeplechase run over 4 miles 514 yards with horses jumping thirty fences over two laps of the course. It is the most valuable jump race in Europe, with the prize fund in 2017 being £1 million.

2. Stanley Park in north Liverpool. Anfield, the home of Liverpool FC, is on one side and Goodison Park, the home of Everton, is on the other.

3. Stockport County's Edgeley Park ground. The River Mersey flows for 27 miles from its origins in Greater Manchester.

4. Bill Shankly in 1981. He was manager of Liverpool Football Club from 1959 to 1974, during which time he transformed their fortunes.

5. Tranmere Rovers.

6. Lancashire County Cricket Team. They play at Liverpool Cricket Club on Aigburth Road in south Liverpool.

7. Everton FC started in 1878. In 1892 they left their Anfield ground after a disagreement with the owner, John Houlding. They moved across Stanley

Park to Goodison Park. Houlding formed Liverpool FC in 1892 to fill his empty ground.

8. The shop is called Everton Two, so the shop's address is Everton Two, Liverpool One. It's another example of the Liverpool sense of humour. Go and have a look.

9. Rugby League in the Super League.

10. The Royal Liverpool Golf Club, Meols Drive in Hoylake (2006 and 2014), and the Royal Birkdale Golf Club, Waterloo Road in Southport (2017).

Tour 16

War and Peace

Liverpool has found itself in the middle of warfare throughout its history and has the scars to show for it. Its sons and daughters have played their part in the world's conflicts. Some of them who were killed have been commemorated in the city or they have lived to tell the tale.

1. The longest battle of the Second World War (1939–45) was the Battle of the Atlantic. This was conducted from underground rooms in Liverpool. Where can you still see these rooms today?

2. The gold from the Bank of England was brought to Liverpool during the Second World War for safe keeping. Where was it stored?

3. Where will you find Liverpool's Cenotaph, the memorial to the dead of both world wars?

4. In the near distance, on William Brown Street you will see something that looks like Nelson's Column. Which war hero does this celebrate?

5. You will find a column supporting a golden flame on the Waterfront near the cruise ship terminal. To whom is this dedicated?

6. The shell of which church stands as a reminder of the bombing of Liverpool in the Second World War?

7. Where will you find the Roll of Honour listing 40,000 soldiers, sailors and airmen from Liverpool who died in the Great War?

8. In 1862 Laird shipbuilders in Birkenhead launched a ship named *Enrica*. Why did this prove to be controversial?

9. By 1643 Liverpool had been captured for Parliament in the English Civil War. Who referred to Liverpool as 'a crow's nest that a parcel of boys could take'? Was he right?

10. The Stanleys are an old Liverpool family who lived in the medieval tower that stood on the Waterfront. How did Lord Thomas Stanley make all the difference to the history of England in 1485?

Answers – Tour 16

1. Western Approaches in Chapel Street, just up from St Nicholas's church. The battle was to keep the shipping lanes across the Atlantic Ocean open. Without these supplies Britain would have starved and lost the war.

2. In the building that was then Martin's Bank in Water Street. You will see the plaque commemorating this on the side of the building in Exchange Street West opposite the Town Hall.

3. On St George's Plateau outside St George's Hall, opposite Lime Street Station.

4. The Duke of Wellington (1769–1852). He led the armies that finally defeated Napoleon at the Battle of Waterloo in 1815. He was also prime minister in 1828–30.

5. Originally intended as a memorial to the engine men who perished on *Titanic* in 1912, by the time it was completed many more engine men had lost their lives in the First World War. Hence, it is dedicated to all 'engine room heroes'. It was unveiled on 8 May 1916.

6. St Luke's church at the top of Bold Street. It was gutted by an incendiary bomb during the May blitz of 1941 and is known locally as 'the bombed-out church'. Its gardens now offer a peaceful retreat.

7. In the war memorial chapel in the north-west transept of Liverpool's Anglican Cathedral. This was dedicated when King George V and Queen Mary visited in 1924 for the consecration of the cathedral.

8. This ship had been built illegally for the Confederate side in the American Civil War. Once safely out of British waters it was renamed *Alabama* and became a notorious raider ship. It took ten Union ships in its first month.

9. It was Prince Rupert who led the King's army and famously looked down on the city from Everton Brow while planning his attack. However, he got a shock because the people of Liverpool put up a much stiffer resistance than he was expecting.

10. He famously changed sides at the Battle of Bosworth Field in 1485. He deserted Richard III and threw his support behind Henry Tudor, a move that proved decisive. His reward was to be created Earl of Derby. The tower is long gone but the Stanleys now live in Knowsley Hall.

Tour 17

Art and Artists

The Liverpool region is the home of many works of art. Some are world famous, others are just fascinating to come across. Some are where you would expect to find them in art galleries and museums, others are in the most unusual places.

1. One of the most recognised pictures is 'Bubbles', the painting by Sir John Everett Millais of his grandson Willie James blowing bubbles. Where will you find it and how did it get there?

2. Where will you find probably the most famous painting of Henry VIII? You will recognise it immediately, it's in all the history books and it's big!

3. Where will you find a 4in bird on a 13ft pole? It is the work of the famous contemporary artist Tracey Emin.

4. What are the strange creatures that you keep bumping into all over the city? They look like a cross between a sheep and a banana.

5. Arthur Dooley, a Liverpool artist, created a very dramatic and challenging statue of 'The Resurrection of Christ' in 1969. It is sometimes known as the 'Black Christ'. Where will you be able to see this?

6. You can't miss the Dazzle Ship in the Canning Graving Dock opposite the Museum of Liverpool, but when did it first appear and why?

7. Where in Liverpool will you be able to see the final work of the renowned sculptor Dame Elizabeth

Frink (1930–93) and a much earlier work by her as well?

8. What is unusual about the paintings by George Stubbs that you will find in the Wedgwood galleries of the Lady Lever Art Gallery in Port Sunlight?

9. 'And when did you last see your father?' This painting about the English Civil War (1642–49) is in all the history books, but it was painted much later, in 1878. Where will you be able to see it today?

10. William Holman Hunt produced an exquisite painting called 'The Finding of the Saviour in the Temple' in 1862. Where is it hidden away in Liverpool?

Answers – Tour 17

1. You will find it in the Lady Lever Art Gallery in Port Sunlight. It is recognised because the Pears company converted it into an advertisement to sell their soap. Lever Brothers bought the Pears company in 1914 and got the painting as well. You will find other paintings in the gallery that were bought to advertise soap.

2. It's in the Walker Art Gallery. It was painted between 1537 and 1547 in the workshop of Hans Holbein. It is difficult to believe that the great master didn't have a hand in it.

3. You will find it as you approach the Anglican Cathedral. It is in front of The Oratory, the perfect Doric temple created by John Foster Junior in 1829. The bird is called 'Roman Standard' and was placed there in 2005 as a tribute to the Liver Bird, the city's mythical symbol.

4. They are Superlambananas. The original one is 17ft tall, yellow and stands in Tithebarn Street. It was created by artist Taro Chiezo for the 1998 ArtTransPennine Exhibition. Some 125 smaller replicas were created in 2008 to mark Liverpool's year as European Capital of Culture.

5. On the side of Princes Park Methodist church on Princes Road, not far from the gates of Princes Park in Toxteth.

6. It appeared on 13 June 2014 as part of the Biennial Contemporary Arts Festival of that year and to mark the centenary of the start of the First World War. The artist Carol Cruz-Diez transformed the Edmund Gardner pilot ship using the kind of camouflage used during the war. By creating an optical illusion the design made it difficult for enemy U-boats to identify and destroy the ship.

7. Her final work is 'Risen Christ' (1993) over the main doors of Liverpool's Anglican Cathedral. It is sometimes known as the 'Welcoming Christ' because his arms are flung open wide welcoming you into the cathedral. Frink also made the beautiful crucifix (1967) over the central altar in the Metropolitan Cathedral.

8. They are painted on ceramic plaques manufactured specially for Stubbs by Josiah Wedgwood. Stubbs was searching for the ideal surface on which to paint that would preserve the original colours. Wedgwood could not resist a challenge. Go and see if he succeeded.

9. In the Walker Art Gallery. See how many other very familiar pictures you can find in this gallery, sometimes called 'The National Gallery of the North'.

10. You'll find it at the Sudley House Gallery in Mossley Hill. The house and the art collection were bequeathed to the city by Emma Holt on her death in 1944. It is a beautiful collection put together by Emma's father. It is a hidden gem not to be missed.

Tour 18

Sons and Daughters of Liverpool

Many women and men from Merseyside or who have been adopted by the region have made a big contribution nationally and internationally. Indeed, the area has produced some of the biggest names in a wide variety of fields and professions. Others have been little known outside the region but have made a big impression locally.

1. It is said you have to be an actor to be a successful politician but who is the only MP to have won two Oscars?

2. Which playwright could be considered to be the original 'Liver Bird'?

3. Which twentieth-century prime minister was brought up in Wirral, served as MP for a Liverpool constituency and awaited the news of his election victories and defeats on election night at the Adelphi Hotel?

4. Liverpool was the first town or city in the UK to appoint a Medical Officer of Health. Who was he?

5. Which of Liverpool's sons was a child prodigy and became a world famous conductor, notably with the Birmingham Symphony Orchestra and the Berlin Philharmonic Orchestra?

6. Which legendary footballer still holds the record for scoring sixty League goals in one football season?

7. Who was born in Ireland, spent most of his life on Merseyside and is buried at the winning post of Aintree Racecourse, where there is also a life-sized statue of him?

8. Who was famous for his paintings of horses, including 'Molly Longlegs' (1761–62) and the book *The Anatomy of the Horse*?

9. In St John's Gardens, behind St George' Hall, two statues of religious men in two warring denominations could claim to have performed their own 'Mersey Miracle' long before Bishop Sheppard and Archbishop Warlock. Who were they?

10. In Basnett Street, between Marks & Spencer and T.K. Maxx, there is a memorial set into the pavement to a fascinating lady called Teddy Dance. Why is she remembered with such affection?

Answers – Tour 18

1. Glenda Jackson, who was born in Birkenhead, was a very successful actress before going into Parliament. She was an MP from 1992 to 2015 and served as Minister for Transport in 1997–99.

2. Carla Lane (1928-2016) who was born in West Derby wrote popular TV series based in Liverpool *The Liver Birds* and *Bread*, as well as *Butterflies*, *No Strings*, *The Mistress* and *I Woke up One Morning*.

3. Harold Wilson (1916–95). He was MP for Huyton in 1945–83, leader of the Labour Party in 1963–76, and prime minister in 1964–70 and 1974–76.

4. Dr William Henry Duncan (1805–63). He was appointed Medical Officer of Health in 1847 after campaigning for better living conditions in the town. He was born at No. 23 Seel Street, which is now the famous Blue Angel Club. The Duncan Building, the teaching block in the Royal Liverpool University Hospital, is named after him.

5. Sir Simon Rattle, born in Liverpool in 1955. He grew up in Mossley Hill and went to school at Liverpool College near Sefton Park.

6. Dixie Dean (1907–80) was born in Birkenhead and specialised in scoring goals with his head. His record came as Everton won the First Division title in the 1927-28 season. See his statue, which was unveiled in 2001 at Goodison Park, Everton's home ground.

7. Red Rum (1965–95), who became famous for his victories at the Grand National, was probably the most famous race horse in the world. He won the race in 1973, 1974 and 1977 and came second in 1975 and 1976.

8. George Stubbs, who was born in Liverpool in 1724. You will find 'Molly Longlegs' as well as 'Horse Frightened by a Lion' (1770) in the Walker Art Gallery. You will find his paintings on enamel in the Lady Lever Art Gallery in Port Sunlight.

9. Monsignor James Nugent (1822–1905) and Canon Thomas Major Lester (1829–1903). One was Roman Catholic, the other Protestant. At a time when there were bloody street fights between the two groups, the two clergymen worked together to improve the lives of destitute children in the city.

10. She was an elegant mature lady who played the piano in the street for four consecutive years (1984–89) to raise money for charity. She raised enormous sums, including £56,000 for a scanner for Clatterbridge Hospital on Wirral, the leading cancer hospital in the region.

Tour 19

Speke Hall

Speke Hall is a sixteenth-century timber-framed Tudor manor house owned by the National Trust and situated near Liverpool John Lennon Airport. It is a haven of peace and tranquillity, where you will be transported back to an earlier age, except during school holidays when it is full of families and children enjoying all sorts of activities organised for them.

1. Where will you encounter Adam and Eve at Speke Hall?

2. Why should you be careful what you say as you stand in front of the original front door to the house, which is on the far side of the courtyard?

3. How do we think they kept a watch on the gatehouse to see who was coming through it in Tudor times?

4. If someone offered to give you a 'Wet Nelly' would you be pleased or frightened?

5. Where will you encounter a giant?

6. The Green bedroom is sometimes called the Priest's Room. How did it get that name?

7. Where will you come face to face with those responsible for the building of the hall?

8. Where will you find valuable original William Morris wallpaper?

9. The stunning stucco ceiling in the Oak Parlour was created in 1608. Why is it sometimes called a 'fruit and nut' ceiling?

10. Why do you cross a bridge to reach the entrance to the house?

Answers – Tour 19

1. These are the two yew trees which are in the courtyard. Adam is believed to be more than 500 years old – that is older than the hall itself.

2. Because you may be being listened to. There is an eavesdrop above the upstairs window to the right of the main door. This is a square hole behind which a servant could crouch in the roof space with his ear to the hole. It was a way of judging whether visitors were friend or foe.

3. In the corner of the Blue Bedroom there is a round hole behind the panelling that would give a view of the gatehouse if there weren't so many bushes and trees in the way today.

4. You would be pleased. It is a traditional Scouse pudding, one of a number of traditional local dishes on offer in the restaurant.

5. In the Great Hall there is a life-sized painting of John Middleton, nicknamed the Childe of Hale. Middleton, who was reputed to be more than 9ft tall, lived in the late sixteenth and early seventeenth centuries.

6. In the corner of the room is a cupboard with a false back. Through this there is a ladder that takes you through a trap door above. From there you need to squeeze through the narrow space between the panelling and the chimney breast into a secret room built into the northern range of the hall. Here a priest could hide while the house was being searched.

7. In the Oak Parlour you will see a carving over the fireplace of the Norris family that was made in the 1560s. You will see Sir William, Edward and Margaret Norris, who had Speke Hall built.

8. In the library and the estate office. It is believed that Frederick Leyland, who rented the hall in 1866–77, was one of William Morris's first customers.

9. The plaster is worked into the shapes of grapes, hazelnuts and pomegranates, as well as lilies and roses. Can you find the two birds hidden in the ceiling?

10. The house was originally surrounded by a moat. You will still see the shape of the moat today on the north and west sides of the house.

Tour 20

Ferry 'Cross the Mersey

A visit to Liverpool is not complete without taking a ferry across the River Mersey. Not only will you have fabulous views of the Liverpool Waterfront but you will discover Birkenhead, which is as fascinating as the city you have just left.

1. When you step off the ferry at Woodside in Birkenhead you will see the U-Boat Story. What's that about?

2. Why will you see tramlines outside the Woodside ferry building?

3. Do you know what is so special about the beautiful Georgian houses in Hamilton Square?

4. Which family had No. 63 Hamilton Square built for them?

5. What was the grand building with the green dome in Hamilton Square until 1974? You can see it from the Liverpool Waterfront across the river.

6. Look for the Wilfred Owen Story, a museum just off Hamilton Square at No. 34 Argyle Street. Why is it here?

7. A couple of doors up from the Wilfred Owen Story is the Rathbone Studio. What famous pottery was made here in 1894–1906?

8. Where in Birkenhead will you find the oldest building on Merseyside?

9. Where in Birkenhead would you have been overawed by the building of the enormous *Ark Royal* aircraft carrier between 1935 and 1937?

10. Birkenhead Park is a beautiful open space designed by Joseph Paxton. Do you know in what way it is also truly historic?

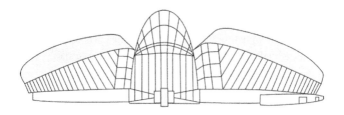

Answers – Tour 20

1. You can explore German U-boat *U-534*, built in 1942, which is now cut into three pieces. It was sunk in May 1945 but forty-nine of the fifty-two crew were rescued. It was brought to the surface in 1993 and has been on display at Woodside since 2007.

2. Birkenhead was the first town in the UK to have horse-drawn trams, in 1860. Although the last tram ran in Birkenhead in 1937 there is a tram museum and sometimes you will see a vintage tram at Woodside.

3. They were designed by James Gillespie Graham, who designed houses in Edinburgh. This 'Scottish' Georgian style is different from the Georgian houses in Liverpool.

4. The Laird family. It was William Laird who bought the land for Hamilton Square and engaged J.G. Graham to design it.

5. This was Birkenhead Town Hall, which was opened in 1887. It ceased to be the town hall when Birkenhead became part of the wider Wirral local authority in 1974.

6. Although he was born in Oswestry, Wilfred Owen spent his formative years in Birkenhead. His father became stationmaster at Birkenhead Woodside Railway Station in 1900.

7. Della Robbia Pottery, inspired by the Florentine sculptor Luca della Robbia. It was founded by Harold Rathbone (1858–1929), a member of the prominent Rathbone family of Liverpool.

8. The ruins of the Priory of St James, which dates from the twelfth century. Although it was closed by order of Henry VIII in the sixteenth century there is still much to see there.

9. Cammell Laird shipyard, next to the Priory. This built ships for the Royal Navy between the 1820s and 1993, and it has since had a rebirth doing ship repairs. You can see the big sheds from the Liverpool Waterfront.

10. It was the first municipal park provided entirely out of public funds, opened on 5 April 1847.

Tour 21

Port Sunlight

Port Sunlight Village is only a short ride away from Liverpool city centre on the Wirral side of the river. However you approach it, by train, bus or car, you will be stunned by the beauty of the village and the immaculately cared for gardens and lawns. If you are guided around the village you will discover the fascinating story of its founders and those who have lived there since its beginnings when the first factory was opened there in 1888.

1. Why can we say that Port Sunlight Village 'was built on soap'?

2. Why don't you see much evidence of washing lines and dustbins as you tour the village?

3. There are more than 900 houses in the village but each block of houses is different. Lever called it the 'charm of irregularity', but there is a unifying style of architecture; what is it?

4. How did the Gladstone Theatre get its name?

5. The house opposite Hulme Hall is known as 'Royal Lodge'. Why?

6. The war memorial is very grand and special. How is it unusual?

7. Port Sunlight is a 'garden village' and the gardens are always very colourful and immaculate. Who looks after them?

8. Why is the statue on the top of the Leverhulme Memorial, alongside the Lady Lever Art Gallery, called 'Inspiration'?

9. Why is Hulme Hall regarded as the 'unlikely but truly historic venue on 18 August 1962 for the real Birth of The Beatles'?

10. Where will you find Lord Leverhulme and his wife Lady Lever today?

Answers – Tour 21

1. It was built for Lever Brothers' workers by William Hesketh Lever and James Darcy Lever. They built up a multinational business that started with the branding and packaging of soap. Their best-known product was Sunlight washing soap.

2. The houses are designed in 'super blocks', mostly oval shaped. The front doors and gardens always face outwards, with the back yards and privies hidden in the middle. Port Sunlight only ever shows you its best side!

3. The style is English Vernacular Revival, which was popular with followers of the Arts and Crafts movement of the late nineteenth century as they looked to the aesthetics of the pre-industrial age.

4. The great Victorian Liberal prime minister William Ewart Gladstone opened it in 1891. William Hesketh Lever was a member of the Liberal Party, serving as Liberal MP for Wirral in 1906-09.

5. In March 1914 King George V and Queen Mary visited Port Sunlight to lay the foundation stone of the Lady Lever Art Gallery. On her ride from the station to Hulme Hall Queen Mary was fascinated

by the houses and asked if she could visit one. They took her across the road from Hulme Hall to No. 20 Bolton Road and the woman who lived there showed her around. The house has been known as Royal Lodge ever since.

6. Its theme is 'Defence of the Home'. This was the theme that Sir William Lever gave to the sculptor Sir William Goscombe John. As well as soldiers and men on it there are also women and children. Local children living in the village were used as models for the bronze figures on the memorial. It was commissioned in 1916 and unveiled in 1921.

7. In Lever's day the company employed gardeners to look after all the gardens. Now they are the responsibility of the Port Sunlight Village Trust, the body set up in 1999 to care for the village.

8. William Hesketh Lever hoped what he aimed to achieve at Port Sunlight to provide a good life for his workers would be an inspiration to others to attempt to do the same. There are four figures in front of the memorial and these represent art, charity, education and industry.

9. This was Ringo Starr's very first public appearance as The Beatles' drummer, thus completing the

legendary line-up of the 'fab four'. This was one of four gigs played by The Beatles at Hulme Hall during 1962.

10. They are buried in the narthex of Christ church, a church built in Port Sunlight by Lever in 1902–04. In the narthex there are monuments designed by William Goscombe John that cover their graves.

Tour 22

Odd Names and Expressions

Liverpool has always had a reputation for its colourful characters. Here are just a few who have left their mark on the city and its fame.

1. Who were known as 'fish and chips' because they were always in the newspapers?

2. Which singer is affectionately known in Liverpool as 'Ar Cilla', although John Lennon always called her Cyril?

3. Who was known as Slaughterhouse Waterhouse?

4. Who became known as the Soap King?

5. Who was Battling Bessie, the poor man's friend?

6. Who invented the Diddymen of Knotty Ash, not to mention Professor Rufus Chuckabutty of Knotty Ash University?

7. Who was the Meccano Man, who gave joy to generations of children and who had a factory in Binns Road from 1914, giving work to between 2,000 and 3,000 people for sixty years?

8. Where will you find the Childe of Hale?

9. Who was the Mole of Edge Hill?

10. Who was Worthless Sidney?

Answers - Tour 22

1. David Sheppard (1929–2005), Bishop of Liverpool in 1975–95, and Derek Worlock (1920–96), Archbishop of Liverpool in 1976–96. They worked together to heal the sectarian divide and as champions of the city. In 1994 they were both awarded the Freedom of the City. The Stephen Broadbent statue of them in Hope Street was unveiled in 2008.

2. Cilla Black, born Priscilla Maria Veronica White, in Scotland Road in 1943. She had No. 1 hits with 'Anyone who had a Heart' and 'You're my World' in 1964. She became a major TV personality, hosting *Blind Date* and *Surprise Surprise!* She died in 2015 and the enduring affection for her in Liverpool was shown by the unveiling of a statue in Mathew Street by her three sons in January 2017.

3. Not a bloodthirsty criminal, but the architect Alfred Waterhouse, who designed some of the outstanding buildings in the city. His chosen building material was often Ruabon brick, which is a vivid red colour, the colour of blood. One such building is the Victoria Building at the top of Brownlow Hill, built in 1889–92. This was the first building of what became the University of

Liverpool. It was one of the new universities that opened at the end of the nineteenth century. This building led to them being called red-brick universities.

4. William Hesketh Lever, Viscount Leverhulme (1851–1925). He was born in Bolton but transformed Bebington on the Wirral into Lever Brothers soap works (now part of the multinational company Unilever) and built Port Sunlight Village for his workers.

5. Bessie Braddock (1899–1970) was a vociferous campaigner as a Labour member of Liverpool City Council, representing St Anne's Ward in 1930–61 and as MP for Liverpool Exchange in 1945–70. There is a blue plaque on her home in Zig Zag Road, West Derby, as well as a statue on the concourse of Lime Street Station.

6. The comedian Sir Ken Dodd, who was born in Knotty Ash in 1927. An irrepressible touring comedian, as well as appearing in numerous TV shows, he is still going strong and about to go into his 90s at the date of publication.

7. Frank Hornby (1863–1936), born at No. 77 Copperas Hill, near the Adelphi Hotel. He was the inventor of the child's educational toy when he

produced Mechanics Made Easy – an Adaptable and Mechanical Toy, which was marketed under the snappier title of Meccano. He eventually diversified into Dinky Toys and Hornby train sets.

8. His grave is in Hale churchyard. He was John Middleton (1578–1623), born in the village of Hale on the outskirts of Liverpool and growing to be 9ft 3in tall. His portrait, actual size but not contemporary, can be seen in Speke Hall.

9. Joseph Williamson 1769–1840. Between about 1805 and 1840 he employed labourers to excavate a mysterious system of tunnels under the area around Smithdown Lane where he lived. No one knows why he built these tunnels, but look out for guided tours that offer a fascinating experience.

10. This was Lord Sydney Beauclerk (1703–44), who married Mary Norris of Speke Hall in 1736. He was the grandson of Charles II and Nell Gwyn and apparently had a reputation for gambling and drinking. You might be able to get a guide at Speke Hall to tell you the grisly ghost story that involves Mary, Sydney and their baby son. Then they will tell you the truth about them, which is even more interesting.

Also in this Series

The Blue Badge Guide's London Quiz Book
978 0 7509 6823 2

Drawing on extensive knowledge and celebrating London's diverse riches, this quiz book invites you to come on a wide-ranging exploration of the megacity the author calls 'the big onion'. Peel away its many layers in the company of one of London's top Blue Badge tourist guides. These twenty-two rounds will inspire you, your family, colleagues and friends to leap from page to pavement in the entertaining company of a local expert. Have fun!